FROM REVIEWS OF THE 2008 PRODUCTION

"It has been a very long time since I've had as much fun at a musical as I had at [Ukulele Land]. I was also unexpectedly touched. And I was thrilled . . . . we can't help but listen and, perhaps, become enlightened and enlarged . . The plot effectively reminds us of the need to be true to ourselves and to question any kind of arbitrary authority, without ever feeling polemical or hackneyed and certainly without resorting to either irony or scare tactics. The activist spirit . . . is strong and authentic, yet it is very gentle. . . . the sometimes pointed, sometimes poetic, always honest lyrics by Jackson, are charming and infectious."
Martin Denton —n*ytheatre.com*

"Never has a musical been so infectiously delightful . . . with jazz legend and ragtime scholar Terry Waldo's amazing compositions, choreographer Celia Rowlson-Hall's campy moves and a cast and chorus that are irresistibly charming in each and every scene, the joy was contagious. . . A spoof on the music industry, our increasingly corporate culture . . . a camp tour-de-force that manages, somehow, to also be steeped in American roots music."
Rayhané S. Sanders —*Show Business Weekly*

"When drug companies take over the world , sex is illegal, so is failure to take your drugs. . . . retro romantic comedy of the future . . . nostalgically inspired lyrics by Jackson particularly *Good Music* [and] *Ukulele Land* . . . it's a Hoot! . . . delightful . . ."
Dan Kassell, Jazz Journalist Association, ***nytimes.com***

"The show is set against the backdrop of a pharmacological dystopia in which The Corporation mandates people take drugs for ailments like sexual desire and the Love Police hunt down illegal monogamous lovers. . . . The mash-up commentary on our overmedicated culture, corporate dominance and ignorance of love and art is a big mandate for the play. Lines like "If this ain't love, Jesse James was a girl" and "Chemical emancipation - that's the new gyration" punctuate its songs with a goofiness that relieves some of that burden. . . . the playful strumming and the endearing innocence of the characters, who dub sex with a loved one 'monogomation', left a mostly optimistic feeling . . . And damned if I wasn't whistling the kitschy, plucky refrain on my way out of the theater."...take a blue bit of sky, put it in your pocket..."
Emily Meredith —*NYPress.com*

". . . this show is this year's jewel in the crown . . . A fast 90 minutes . . . charms with ease, rightly wearing its limited ambitions as a badge of honor: to provide a little musical entertainment in a troubled world."
Christopher Murray —***Back Stage***

"Finally, the poodle of the guitar world gets some respect when a plucky band of ukulele strummers defy the authorities in the music deprived, sexless future of Uke Jackson (book and lyrics) and composer Terry Waldo's dystopian musical comedy."
Time Out NY

Ukulele Land is published in the United States of America by Uke Jackson Entertainment, PO Box 492, Delaware Water Gap, Pennsylvania 18327

Ukulele Land copyright © 2011 by Uke Jackson
The copyright for the book and lyrics of **Ukulele Land** is solely and wholly owned by the author. Any reproduction in any format, print or electronic, now in existence or as yet unknown, without the express written permission of the author is forbidden. All rights for adaptations of any kind for any medium, already in existence or yet to be invented, are reserved and can only be granted by the author or his heirs or assigns, for the term of the copyright.

Ukulele Land is a work of fiction. Names, characters, places and incidents are either the product of the author's imagination or are used fictitiously. Any resemblance to actual persons, living or dead, events, or locations is entirely coincidental.

Purchase or possession of this readers' edition of the book and lyrics for **Ukulele Land** in no way conveys the rights to produce the show for the stage or any other medium. Nor does it in any way convey the rights to any of the music. For information regarding production rights, please convey your inquiry via post to Uke Jackson Entertainment, PO Box 492, Delaware Water Gap, Pennsylvania 18327 or by email to ukejackson@ukejackson.com

FIRST EDITION

ISBN-13: 978-0615433059
ISBN-10: 0615433057

Cover design and book design by
Charles de Bourbon, BGAstudios.com

www.ukejackson.com

UKULELE LAND
Book and lyrics for a musical comedy

A NOTE FROM THE AUTHOR

In 2008, *Ukulele Land* was showcased in a production in the East Village on the island of Manhattan. At that time, the title was *Sex! Drugs! & Ukuleles!* – which was pushed on me and which I used against my better judgment. So, I have since restored the original title.

In this readers' version, my ideal sets are described. In the barebones production, there were no huge Tiki figures rising from the stage, breathing smoke while eyes glowed red. The set then was static, with a large red corporate © as the only set piece.

That show got good (if not great) reviews. However, the economy was collapsing. For whatever reasons, at that time, there was little enthusiasm from producers for a musical comedy about a pharmacologically-controlled corporate police state, regardless of notices.

The music for the show was composed by Terry Waldo, one of America's more under-appreciated musical geniuses. We wrote the songs during a six-week stint. Working with Terry so closely was a high point for me as both musician and playwright. He seemed to be connected to some music pipeline that allowed him to come up with melody after melody, tune after tune. Someday, perhaps, there will be a cast album once a more complete production is mounted. In the meantime, if one is so inclined, bits and pieces of the music from the showcase can be found on the internet.

After the production closed, and a few months passed, I went back to the script and did some rewriting. I revised some lyrics. One song was cut. Another song that had been cut was restored, and a new tune was added. I also restored some storytelling that had been inadvertently dropped during rehearsals, along with a much-needed intermission.

Even though this readers' edition is without music, the words do tell a story. It is meant as a cautionary tale. In writing *Ukulele Land*, I attempted to use the future as a mirror for the present.

Since the showcase production, several people who saw it have said to me that it seems every day America, and the world, are becoming more and more like the future portrayed in the musical. Even I was shocked when a primary conglomeration of mental health professionals recently announced that hundreds of new "syndromes" were being added to their handbook – a move gleefully applauded by the pharmaceutical industry.

It is my desire and hope that someday, somewhere a producer -- not-for-profit or commercial -- who still believes in the transforming power of theater will choose to mount a new production of this show, regardless of how much corporate muckety-mucks may cringe.

Until that event comes to pass, I hope you enjoy reading this, the book and lyrics for *Ukulele Land*.

Uke Jackson
Delaware Water Gap, PA
January 2011

The original cast in the 2008 production:

JULIE.. Meg Cavanaugh
LIZ .... Lindsay Foreman
MAX .... John Forkner
PETE .... Andrew Guilarte

CHORUS
(Corporate Security, Love Police, hula dancers, etc.)

Mia Breaux
Tammy Carrasco
Jenna Fakhoury
Dustin Flores
Kristen Lewis
Guy Lockard

Victor Maog directed the 2008 production.
Celia Rowlson-Hall was the choreographer.

MUSICIANS

Terry Waldo (composer) .... piano
John Gill .... percussion
Samantha Ryan ....substitute pianist
Kevin Dorn...............................substitute drummer

CREW
David Alpert was the Production Stage Manager.
Michael Jarett was the lighting designer.
Susan Gittens was the costume designer.
Nancy Vitale was the production supervisor.
Janice A. Lee was a music consultant.
Jonathan Slaff was the press agent.
Daniel Kohler engineered the sound.

Ukulele Land
is dedicated to
freedom-loving musicians everywhere.

DRAMATIS PERSONAE

VOTA – Voice of the Author (*a woman's voice, heard but not seen*)
Max – young ukulele player
Liz – young ukulele player
Julie – young ukulele player
Pete – a mysterious stranger with secrets
Captain of the Guard -- a non-singing heavy
Chorus of Singing Dancers – at a ratio of 2 women for every man, these players portray the Love Police, Corporate Security, hula dancers, corporate dancers, etc.

SETTING

The play is set at the end of the 21st century, though VOTA (*a female voice*) narrates during the action/dance of the prologue, as though from the viewpoint of the 22nd century. An environmental catastrophe, referred to in passing as "the Great Emergency," led to the entire planet being ruled by the One World Corporation. Much of what might be considered normal behavior today is considered abnormal in this future. Most abnormal behavior is treated with drugs. There are laws against drug evasion.

Among other things, all public performance and/or electronic dissemination of music is illegal unless it is a product of the talents of The Corporation's Top Ten musical acts. Sex and love are also illegal.

SCENE LOCATIONS

A city street, an abandoned warehouse, a park at night, an abandoned farm house, an audition stage, corporate offices

PROLOGUE and OVERTURE

SONG: **Instrumental Overture/Fanfare**

VOTA: At the end of the 21st Century, the planet was a much different place than it is now. The Great Emergency, an environmental and financial collapse, was the result of more than a century of evil economic philosophy that can be summed up as "Burn it and we will profit." This philosophy benefited an elite few. The endless pollution and war that resulted from this greedy construct was exacerbated by exponential population growth. The Great Emergency lasted from 2038 until 2074. It ended with the One World Pharmaceutical Corporation controlling everything everywhere. Much of what we now consider normal behavior was considered abnormal under the Corporation.

> *A large red © on white background appears center stage.*

All abnormal behavior was treated pharmaceutically. Drug evasion was forbidden. History was erased at every turn. Sex was illegal. Procreation was generated in laboratories run by the corporation.

> *Coinciding with the speech, two Lovers are embracing. A sharp buzz sounds. Members of the Love Police enter, rush across the stage and begin pummeling and separating the lovers, who are dosed with a pharmaceutical, and dragged offstage.*

Children were raised in corporate controlled pods. And making music was illegal unless you were a member of the corporate Top 10. Then, at the end of the 21st century, three young outlaw ukulele players changed everything. This is their story.

Chorus enters, sings and acts out the song.

SONG: ***THERE ARE MEDS***

CHORUS:
>THERE ARE MEDS THAT YOU TAKE FOR WORRY,
>THERE ARE MEDS THAT YOU TAKE FOR PAIN.
>THERE'S A MED WHEN YOU NEED TO HURRY,
>OR TO LOSE ALL THAT WEIGHT AGAIN.
>THERE ARE MEDS TO CURE SEXUAL URGE,
>THERE ARE MEDS TO MAKE YOU SIT VERY STILL.

>>*Max enters and slips thru the chorus toward Liz, who enters and moves toward him. Max passes Liz a slip of paper.*

>THERE'S A MED THAT WILL QUICKLY PURGE
>THE URGE TO GO AGAINST THE CORPORATE WILL.

>>*Julie enters.*

JULIE:
>PILLS, TABLETS, CAPSULES, INJECTIONS
>THERE ARE MEDS TO PUT HAIR ON YOUR PATE.

>>*Julie begins dispensing meds to the Chorus, who receive with hands cupped together, or by sticking out their tongue, and consuming their doses like a form of communion. With a hypo, Julie wags her finger in a scold at the Last in Line (LiL), who turns around and bends at the waist. Julie injects LiL in the hip. LiL jerks up straight, walks stiff-legged, robotic. Stops and turns, sings with All. Then LiL continues slow progress to an Exit point.*

JULIE:
    WE HAVE DRUGS THAT ONLY SERVE REPRESSION
ALL:
    BUT NO MED CAN UNDO YOUR FATE

Liz crosses to Julie thru the Chorus. Liz slips Julie the piece of paper.

    THERE ARE MEDS THAT MAKE YOU HAPPY,
    THERE ARE MEDS THAT MAKE YOU DULL,
JULIE:
    YOU CANNOT ESCAPE YOUR DUTY,
ALL:
    TAKE YOUR MEDS FOR THE GOOD OF US ALL.

End of song

Chorus exits. Last in Line's movement should make her last to exit, as Julie reads the note from Liz and Max, then tears the piece of paper into tiny bits and lets them drift from her hand -- they should shimmer in the light -- as she exits.

ACT ONE

ACT ONE
SCENE 1: AN ABANDONED WAREHOUSE

Lights up on Max and Liz, their ukuleles in hand. Then Julie enters in a rush, looking over her shoulder. She carries a cloth bag with the Corporate © emblazoned on it.

JULIE: They know about us!
MAX: Calm down. They're looking for drug evaders.
JULIE: If we get caught playing music, they'll run us in.
LIZ: I hate these security pushes. Why's it happening now?
MAX: Drug evasion is rampant. That's what the alert said.
LIZ: Can you blame people? The corporation announces a new syndrome and a new med almost every week. Who can keep up?
JULIE: Some people really need their meds.
MAX: But most don't, and you know it. How did laughing out loud in public become the LOL syndrome?
LIZ: You don't have to justify your job dispensing meds, Julie. Everybody has to do something.

Sirens fill the air, rising in volume as though getting closer. Julie clutches Max's arm. Liz grabs his other arm. Alarm bells ring. Then the bells stop ringing. The sirens fade away into the night outside.

MAX: Let's play some music!
LIZ: I'm ready. Let's kick it.

SONG: *TIME TO FLY*

MAX, JULIE, & LIZ:
> TAKE THE BLUE FROM THE SKY,
> PUT IT IN YOUR POCKET.
> TAKE YELLOW FROM THE SUN,
> FUEL UP THE ROCKET.
> WE'RE GONNA SOAR OUT THERE.
> MAKE ALL THE PEOPLE CARE,
> IT'S TIME TO FLY,
> IT'S TIME TO FLY.
>
> WHEN THERE'S TRUTH IN YOUR SONG,
> NO ONE CAN STOP YOU.
> IT SWINGS YOU RIGHT ALONG
> 'TIL NO ONE CAN TOP YOU.
> PUT CHANCE IN YOUR ROMANCE,
> MAKE EV'RYBODY DANCE.
> IT'S TIME TO FLY,
> IT'S TIME TO FLY.
>
> THERE ARE SONGS TO SING,
> THERE ARE CROWDS TO WOW,
> THERE ARE BELLS TO RING,
> AND IT ALL STARTS NOW.
> WE'LL FLY ON A CLOUD
> AND FLOAT ON A BREEZE,
> SING SONGS OUT LOUD
> WHENEVER WE PLEASE.
>
> TAKE THE BLUE FROM THE SKY,
> PUT IT IN YOUR POCKET.
> TAKE YELLOW FROM THE SUN,
> FUEL UP THE ROCKET.
> GO SO HIGH AND GO SO FAST,
> MAKE THE FEELING LAST.

IT'S TIME TO FLY,
IT'S TIME TO FLY.
End of song

MAX: I have to say it -- we are really getting good.
LIZ: We should audition for the Top Ten! And get those amazing golden jumpsuits!

Max and Julie roll their eyes.

LIZ: I'm serious. We should.
JULIE: The Top Ten auditions are fixed, Liz. Everybody knows that.
LIZ: That's what everybody says. But nobody knows for sure.

Max and Julie shake their heads in disbelief at Liz's relentless optimism. Pete enters.

PETE: Go for it. Reach for the stars. You're good enough. You've dreamt it. Now -- do it.

Liz and Julie start at the sound of Pete's voice.

MAX: It's an Edger! Liz, get away from him! Do you want to get contaminated?

Pete crosses to the Trio. He is dressed in rags but he looks like a shaman.

PETE: Maybe I'm not the edge but the center, youngster. I love love love the sound of ukulele music. Actually, I'm surprised you even know what a ukulele is.
LIZ: Uke's are small and light and easy to hide, and the strings last forever.
MAX: Yeah. They're the outlaws' choice.

JULIE: Outlaw?! Don't say that, Max. It sounds terrible. You don't know who he is!
PETE: Music is food for the soul, and yours is a very good meal.
LIZ: We should listen to him. We should go for it! We need to be part of the Big Time! Imagine us in golden jumpsuits!
MAX: Listening to him sounds like a bad idea to me.
PETE: Oh really? A bad idea? Tell me more.
MAX: Well, um, well, look at you. You're an edger, a bum.
PETE: What if I was to tell you I'm a magic man?
MAX: I'd ask you why you're living in an abandoned storage facility?

> *Booming sound of a metal door opening is heard. Pete disappears into the shadows. Dancers dressed in tight, corporate security uniforms with exaggerated crimson epaulets, and a matching red corporate logo on their chests. They march in lockstep.*

LIZ: Corporate security!
MAX: This way --come on!

> *Max, Liz and Julie stash their instruments in their cloth corporate shopping bags as they exit running.*
> *Music rising—military-like drums as the dancers march to the front of the stage. They stop in unison.*
> *Pete emerges from the shadows dressed in a golden jumpsuit. He sniffs each of his own shoulders in succession and wrinkles his nose as he crosses to the line of dancers. Captain of the Guard starts at the appearance of Pete.*

CAPTAIN OF THE GUARD: (*startled*) Where did you come from?
PETE: Before you were here, I was here.
CAPTAIN: I can see that. But why are you here?
PETE: Are you interrogating me?
CAPTAIN: No, sir.
PETE: Good. Now let's all sing the corporate anthem shall we?
CAPTAIN: Right here? Right now?
PETE: Right here, right now. Absolutely. Is that a problem?
CAPTAIN: No sir.

SONG: ***THE CORPORATE ANTHEM***

PETE & DANCERS:
>THE CORPORATION IS HERE FOR US,
>THE CORPORATION ENDED FEAR FOR US.
>THE WORLD WAS A DANGEROUS PLACE
>'TIL THE CORPORATION
>SAVED THE HUMAN RACE.
>WE ARE THE CHILDREN
>OF THE CORPORATION,
>THE WORLD IS ONE
>BIG CORPORATE NATION.
>THE CORPORATION KNOWS
>WHAT'S BEST FOR US,
>EXECUTIVES CONTROL THE REST OF US.
>THE CORPORATION MAKES US STRONG,
>IT GIVES US LIFE AND WE LIVE LONG.
>MEDS AND HOME AND EVEN SONG,
>THE CORPORATION DOES NO WRONG.
>THE CORPORATION IS HERE FOR US,
>THE CORPORATION ENDED FEAR FOR US.
>WE ARE GUIDED BY THE LAW,
>THE CORPORATION SAVED US ALL!
>   *End of song*

SCENE 2: A PARK
Max and Julie sit on a park bench.

JULIE: I hope they caught that edger. He really needs treatment.
MAX: Always on the job --that's my Julie.

> *Max pulls her close for an attempted kiss. Julie pushes Max away.*

JULIE: (*offended*) I'm not always on the job. Don't you think it was obvious? That man isn't living at the edge, he's living beyond it, way beyond. Corporate security would be doing him a favor, getting him to a clinic.
MAX: Maybe all he needs is love.
JULIE: Love? Hah!
MAX: He did like our music.
JULIE: You too now? An Edger claps his hands and you're ready to jump? You and Liz would make a perfect couple.
MAX: Liz and me? Hey, I like you, Julie. You're my girl.
Here's how it is.

> *Max reaches into his cloth bag sitting beside the bench, takes out his uke and begins to sing to Julie. She rolls her eyes and shakes her head—mocking, but bemused. Max sings:*

SONG: ***WHERE LOVE MUST START***

MAX:
> IT MAY BE WRONG,
> BUT FOR YOU I LONG.
> MY LOVE FOR YOU IS SO REAL.
> THERE'S NO DENYING

YOUR LOVE SENDS ME FLYING,
PLEASE HEAR MY HEARTFELT APPEAL.

WHEN I'M ALONE WITHOUT YOU,
TIME MOVES SLOWLY FOR ME.
I WANT TO KNOW YOUR SWEETEST CHARMS,
IN YOUR LOVING ARMS I SHOULD BE.

> *Liz enters on opposite side of the stage. Max moves toward Liz and sings to her as lights on Julie fade.*

LOVE IS THE FIRE,
HEAT'S MY DESIRE.
I PRAY WE'LL NOT BE APART.
PLEASE HEAR MY PLEAS.
IN YOUR HEART I MUST BE.
LET ME LIVE WHERE LOVE MUST START.
End of song

MAX: I wrote that for you.
LIZ: No song is for only one person. Like no person is for only one person.
MAX: What if you really only love one person?
LIZ: Nobody loves just one person. That kind of love is illegal, remember?
MAX: So what if it's illegal? Music is illegal, too.
LIZ: Only until we're in the Top 10.

> *Max rolls his eyes. Liz sings:*

SONG: ***TOP TEN***

LIZ:

TOP TEN! TOP TEN!
WE'RE GOING TO THE TOP AND THEN

EVERYONE WILL HEAR OUR SONGS
AGAIN AND AGAIN AND AGAIN
TOP TEN! TOP TEN!
THERE'LL BE NO STOPPING US WHEN
SUCCESS IS OURS AND WE STARS
AND WE'LL BE THERE 'TIL THE END

> *Max exits.*
> *Liz crosses as lights come up on Julie.*

TOP TEN! TOP TEN!
LET THE MUSIC BE YOUR FRIEND
WE'RE GONNA CLIMB THE CHARTS,
HAVE MORE THAN WE CAN SPEND
TOP TEN! TOP TEN!
OUR MUSIC WILL SET A NEW TREND!
WE CAN CHANGE THE WHOLE WIDE WORLD
AND PUT IT ON THE MEND

LIZ & JULIE:
TOP TEN! TOP TEN!
WE'RE GOING TO THE TOP AND THEN
EVERYONE WILL HEAR OUR SONGS
AGAIN AND AGAIN
TOP TEN! TOP TEN!
THERE'LL BE NO STOPPING US WHEN
SUCCESS IS OURS AND WE ARE STARS
AND WE'LL BE THERE 'TIL THE END!
End of song

JULIE: (*laughs*) Okay, Liz, I can't argue with you any longer. You win.
LIZ: (*delighted*) So we'll do it? Together? The three of us? We'll go for it? We'll try out for the Top 10?
JULIE: I can't speak for Max, but you can count me in.

LIZ: (*grabs Julie by the arm, fervent*) Julie, we're going to make it. I can feel it. We're going to take a stand. We're going to show the Corporation what we can do. It's going to be great. We're great. So it's got to be great for us.

JULIE: We can't practice near that crazy edger anymore, though. There's someone who really is in need of meds! He makes me all nervous.

LIZ: I think he's hot, and I think you think so too.

JULIE: Hot?! He's an edger!

LIZ: So what? There's something about him. And he called himself a magic man. What's that mean?

JULIE: He is intriguing, isn't he? The way he talks gives me chills – even though he's clearly got problems.

LIZ: I knew it! (*pause*) So, did Max sing you his new love song?

JULIE: Oh, he sang it. He sang it to you, too, huh? Did he write it "just for you?"

LIZ & JULIE: (*sing*)
   LET ME LIVE WHERE LOVE MUST START.

JULIE (*laughing*) That's it. He's so sentimental sometimes.

LIZ: Sentimental, yes. Truthful? That's a whole other conversation. (*pause*) How about you? Are you going to sleep with him?

JULIE: With Max? No way.

LIZ: I might -- someday, if the opportunity ever arises.

JULIE: Oh, if I know Max, it will arise.

> *Sound of feet marching is heard. Both Liz and Julie react with fear.*

JULIE: Oh no! What time is it? Here comes a curfew patrol. Let's get out of here!

LIZ: Go!

UKULELE LAND

*Liz and Julie exit in a dash.
Love Police march on stage carrying nightsticks and as a chorus they sing.*

SONG: ***LOVE POLICE***

LOVE POLICE:
>WE ARE THE LOVE POLICE
>WE ARE THE LOVE POLICE
>GOT TO TAKE YOU IN
>STOP YOUR STICKY SIN
>DON'T YOU DARE TO MASTURBATE
>OR COPULATE OR EVEN MATE
>
>CHEMICAL EMANCIPATION
>THAT IS THE NEW GYRATION

>*The Love Police begin to pull Lovers from the shadows two by two and beat them with nightsticks in a violent ballet.*

WE ARE THE LOVE POLICE
WE ARE THE LOVE POLICE
GOT TO TAKE YOU IN
STOP YOUR STICKY SIN
NOW YOU MUST CONFESS
WHY THIS KINKY MESS?
WHY WERE YOU UNDRESSED?
SO UNDRESSED
SO UNDRESSED

CHEMICAL EMANCIPATION
THAT IS THE NEW GYRATION
WE ARE THE LOVE POLICE
WE ARE THE LOVE POLICE
>*End of song*

SCENE 3: THE WAREHOUSE
Max, Liz, and Julie are all in the warehouse.

SONG: ***GOOD MUSIC***

MAX, JULIE, & LIZ: (*play ukes and sing*)
GIVE US A SONG, ANY SONG,
WE'LL TAKE UP OUR UKES
AND SWING IT ALONG.
PASSING CHORDS, PICKING LEAD,
SCRUBBING A BEAT, TAPPING OUR FEET.

GOOD MUSIC IT CAN KEEP YOU ALIVE,
NOW LISTEN TO ME THAT AIN'T NO JIVE.
GOOD MUSIC CAN BE
BETTER THAN MAKIN' LOVE.

THERE'S A FEELING IN EV'RY HEART.
COMES ALIVE WHEN THE MUSIC STARTS,
MAKES FACES SMILE,
JUST LIKE THE STARS UP ABOVE,

OH BABY, LET'S PLAY A TUNE
FOR SWINGIN' AND DANCIN' NOW
LET'S SING A SONG ABOUT
 TAKIN' A CHANCE AND HOW.

LIZ:
COME ON SISTER
MAX, JULIE, & LIZ:
IT DON'T MATTER IF IT'S SLOW OR FAST.
THAT MUSIC MAKES THE GOOD TIMES LAST.
CAN'T GET ENOUGH
OF THAT WONDERFUL STUFF
SO LET'S PLAY.

GOOD MUSIC CAN BE SOFT AND SWEET,

UKULELE LAND

OR IT CAN GET YOU UP ON YOUR FEET.
THAT MUSIC IS A SUPER TREAT FOR ME.
THAT MUSIC MAKE YOU SING AND DANCE

MAX:
IT CAN EVEN MAKE YOU DROP YOUR PANTS.

MAX, JULIE, & LIZ:
FOLKS ENJOYIN' MUSIC
WHAT A MARVELOUS SIGHT TO SEE.
COME ON NOW.
GOOD MUSIC HOW I LOVE IT SO.
IT'S THE BEST THING IN THE WORLD I KNOW.
LET'S HAVE MUSIC,
COME ON AND BRING IT HOME TO ME.
End of song

JULIE: Do you always have to sing about dropping your pants?

Pete's voice booms from the shadows.

PETE: I'm here! Glad I got back in time to hear that. I'm thoroughly impressed. You three are first rate. And you're just about ready.
MAX: Ready for what?
PETE: Your audition. The Top 10 -- Fame and riches and freedom to do whatever you want. Yep. You're on your way. Though you sure don't want to play that song for the executives. No no no no.
MAX: Thanks for the opinion, but I think we can decide for ourselves what songs we play. And forget about any auditions. Right now the majority vote is that we will not audition.
JULIE: Max, that's something we have to talk about.
LIZ: We can't go on like this. We'll get caught eventually, if not sooner.

MAX: Whoa! Slow down now, ladies. I thought we were agreed. I can't believe this. You two turned on me!
LIZ and JULIE: Turned on you?!?!
PETE: Would you mind saving your squabbling for later?
JULIE: Excuse me? Would you remind me who asked for your opinion?
PETE: Hey! I'm trying to help you.
MAX: Just what we need -- help from an edger. Julie, next time we hook up here, snag a few meds from your job and bring them along? We'll hold this guy down and give him some of the help he needs.
PETE: Fine! Have it your way. Go try out for the Top 10 without Pete's help. You'll get nowhere but flat on your back with a drip in your arm. You see, I have the key.

A cymbal sounds. Pete turns to leave.

LIZ: Wait, please. I want to hear what you have to say.
MAX: Liz, let him go. What can he possibly tell us?

Pete stops and turns.

PETE: I can tell you so much your head would spin right off (*drums*) and go shooting up to the moon. I can tell you a place where we can go to prepare you for the Top 10 without anybody bothering us.
MAX: You're not one of us - all you're doing is bothering us.
PETE: I'm talking about a place where there's plenty of space and no one will bother you.
MAX: And how far away is this mythical place?
PETE: Not so far as you think.

MAX: Uh huh... This is all very interesting, Pete, especially considering the source.
PETE: What's that supposed to mean?
MAX: You're a total edger. Crawl back into the shadows and leave us alone. We don't need you or your advice.
LIZ: Max! You don't have to be mean.
JULIE: Pharma treatment is free for someone in your condition.
PETE: (*outraged*) Someone in my condition?!? That's it! This has gone on long enough. It's time for you to know the truth about Pete.

> *Music rises as Pete grabs at his clothes with both hands and rips away his rags. They fall to the floor and Pete steps out of them, dressed in a metallic golden rock star jumpsuit bearing the corporate © logo.*
> *The trio is bug-eyed and agape.*

PETE: Now hear this, youngsters. I was in the Top 10. I was there, right at the top, again and again, and I'm going to take you to the top. So drop the sarcasm, lose the attitude, and get ready to swing. Go pack your necessities and meet me back here in two hours. I'll arrange transport in the meantime.
LIZ: Transport? Where are we going? For how long? We can't just go away. I have a job. We all have jobs.
MAX: (*slightly dazed*) Wow. This is too strange. I'm not sure anymore what's going on here. You're wearing the golden jumpsuit. The Top Ten golden jumpsuit.
JULIE: Wow!

> *Julie crosses to Pete and strokes his arm.*

PETE: I know what I'm wearing.

Pete slips his arm around Julie's waist.

JULIE: Wow!
PETE: We're skipping town, as they used to say. We're getting your act together and taking it to the hills. Now, go get ready. You saw corporate security come in here the other night. Do you want to stand around until they come again?
JULIE: (*completely dazed*) Wow! Wow!
PETE: No time to wait. You're going to Ukulele Land.
MAX, LIZ, & JULIE: Ukulele Land?
LIZ: Is there really such a place?
PETE: Ukulele Land is a uketopia where your creativity -- all three of you -- shall flourish. It's filled with sights, sounds, tastes, and experiences all guaranteed to make your music thrilling. Ukulele Land is hillbilly heaven! Give me a vamp in F, please.

> *Max plays a vamp and intro. The large round red Corporate © backdrop flies out.*

SONG: ***UKULELE LAND***

PETE:

> UKULELE LAND, THAT'S THE PLACE TO BE.
> UKULELE LAND, ALL YOUR CARES WILL FLEE.
> HOT PEPPER CHILI AND HAWAIIAN SHIRTS.
> UKULELE LAND, WHERE LOVE NEVER HURTS.

> *Neon palm trees, sun, argon clouds light up the backdrop. Two huge Tiki figures with glowing red eyes, breathing smoke, rise from the stage. The words UKULELE LAND start flashing in neon on backdrop. Dancers in grass skirts and leis, and not much else, enter and begin to dance and sing harmony.*

UKULELE LAND

UKULELE LAND, SKIES ARE ALWAYS BLUE,
UKULELE LAND, FRIENDS ARE ALWAYS TRUE.
FREEDOM RINGS OUT DAILY,
FROM EV'RY UKULELE.
UKULELE LAND, THAT'S THE PLACE TO BE.

UKULELE LAND, FIRES ON THE BEACH.
UKULELE LAND, NOTHING'S OUT OF REACH.
YOU'LL LEARN GIN RUMMY
AND GORGE AT HOT CLAM BAKES,
PLAYING UKULELE,
THAT'S ALL THAT IT TAKES.

UKULELE LAND, DANCING IN GRASS SKIRTS.
ALL THAT YOU CAN EAT
OF THOSE CHOC'LATE DESSERTS.
SLEEP ALL DAY, NIGHTS RUN WILD,
YOU WILL FIND YOUR INNER CHILD.
UKULELE LAND,
THAT'S WHERE YOU'LL WANNA BE,

MAX: (*interrupting*) We're doomed.

Neon lights flicker and go out.

PETE: You're not doomed!
MAX: There's no such place.
PETE: Just do what I say and everything will be great. Meet me back here in two hours with all you need to escape.
MAX, LIZ, & JULIE: Escape?!?
PETE: Better go get ready. (*to Chorus*) All together now.

Pete raises his arms like a conductor. The trio exits. Neon lights brighten on back drop again.

Chorus and Pete begin singing the third verse.

PETE & CHORUS:
>UKULELE LAND, CROWDS ALL SING ALONG
>UKULELE LAND, YOU'LL KNOW EVERY SONG.
>ALL KINDS OF DANCERS
>SWINGIN' CHEEK TO CHEEK,
>YOU CAN EVEN EARN
>A MILLION BUCKS A WEEK.
>
>UKULELE LAND, EV'RYONE IS KIND,
>PLAY THAT UKULELE,
>NOT A SOUL WILL MIND.
>STRUM THAT UKULELE
>AND SING YOUR LOVE SONGS GAILY.
>UKULELE LAND, THAT'S THE PLACE TO BE.
>>*End of song*

SCENE 4: **AN ABANDONED FARM**

Two weeks later. A ramshackle farm house is suggested in the background. A broken down split rail fence is off to one side. Liz and Julie are dressed in bright, skimpy sundresses. The scene is punctuated with animal and insect noises.

JULIE: This is Ukulele Land? I can't believe this is happening. We're done. Finished. We've become edgers, and all thanks to Pete.
LIZ: I believe in Pete. You saw his golden jumpsuit!
JULIE: Liz, will you please forget the jumpsuit!?! Who cares about a stupid golden jumpsuit?
LIZ: The jumpsuit was real!
JULIE: Oh what's the use!?! The corporation will put us on an eternal meds regimen. I can't believe we let this happen. We're trapped.
LIZ: I wouldn't say we're trapped exactly. Abandoned would be more accurate. And Pete could still come back. It hasn't been that long. I don't get it. Didn't I see you kissing him goodbye?
JULIE: So what if I kissed him? I was just being friendly. Back then I still believed in his jumpsuit. (*wails*) It's been two whole weeks. Where could he possibly be?
LIZ: It's really not that bad, Julie. There's plenty of food, and the music is going great. We're all together, and at least we don't have to hide to practice our songs. Two weeks isn't that long.
JULIE: How long do you think we can stay here like this? Cut off. Abandoned. Living like edgers in this horrible place.
LIZ: It's not so bad.

Liz puts her arm around Julie's shoulder to try and comfort her.

JULIE: Not so bad?!? It's completely unhealthy. It's dusty, it's musty, and there's a mouse! The only reason you like it is because you and Max are having sex all day. It's terrible! It's all terrible.
LIZ: Max and I being monogamous is terrible?
JULIE: No! That's not what I meant! Everything else. It's all terrible!
LIZ: Everything, Julie? Come on. At least these vintage clothes are fun.
JULIE: I would gladly trade them for a chance to sneak home. What will our Pods and Nods think when we're caught?
LIZ: Max says the three of us could be monogamous together. Would that make you happier?
JULIE: Are you kidding me?

Max enters. He wears a bright vintage Hawaiian shirt and faded blue jeans.

JULIE: (*sarcastic*) Here he is now – the great monogamous outlaw himself.
MAX: Oh, she told you. Well, what do you think?
JULIE: What do I think?
MAX: Yes. What do you think about the three of us? Not right now, though. I just saw a huge fat fish in the creek. I want to rig up a way to catch him.
LIZ: I saw lines and poles and hooks in that storage shed, but it all looks kind of primitive.
MAX: (*vigorously*) I like primitive.
JULIE: (*wails*) Oooooohhh.
MAX: That's what you think -- Ooooooohh?
JULIE: What am I supposed to think? Do you two even know what monogamous means?

LIZ: Oh, Max knows how to monogamate.

Julie collapses sobbing.

MAX: Now what?
LIZ: All she can think about is getting back to corporate civilization.
MAX: Back? Why? This place is perfect.
JULIE: (*wails even more loudly*) OOOOOOHHH!!
MAX: (*ignores Julie*) I've been working on a song about it. I'll play it for you. Give me a second.

> *Max grabs a ukulele, tunes. Liz stands up, extends a hand to Julie.*

LIZ: Come on, sweetie. Get up. Sitting all hunched over isn't helping your attitude.

> *Julie looks up longingly at Liz.*

JULIE: I want meds. I want to feel better. I want to feel happy.

> *Liz continues to hold out her hand. She beckons with twiddling fingers.*

LIZ: Come on, Julie. You don't need meds. All you need is to play some music . . .
JULIE: No!
LIZ: . . . take a walk . . .
JULIE: (*plaintive*) No!
LIZ: . . . eat some food.

> *Julie takes Liz's hand and gets her to her feet.*

JULIE: No more beans! Please! No more beans out of a can!

LIZ: Okay. No more beans. Not for a couple days anyway. Pete did stock the place with food for us. So maybe we're not really abandoned.

JULIE: Where are the clam bakes and pinochle games? Where's Ukulele Land?

LIZ: Maybe it's gone -- Part of Chemical Emancipation?

JULIE: Where are all the mountain Williams?

LIZ: Mountain Williams?

MAX: I think she means hillbillies.

> *Max positions himself to serenade the girls. He begins with a flourish across the strings.*

MAX: Okay. Here it is. (*begins strumming, singing*)

SONG: ***WINTER ON A MOUNTAIN SIDE*** (*fragment*)

MAX:
    SPENDIN' WINTER ON A MOUNTAIN SIDE,

JULIE: (*interrupting loudly*) Winter?!

MAX: (*continues singing, oblivious*)
    IN A HOUSE THAT'S WARM AND WIDE.
    JUST THE THREE OF US, SIDE BY SIDE...

> *Julie springs into action, rushing toward Max with her hands ready to strangle him.*

JULIE: I'm going to kill him!

> *Max stops playing, shocked.*

LIZ: Julie, no!

> *Julie almost gets her hands around Max's throat, but Liz gets her arms around Julie and holds her back as she struggles, then begins sobbing, collapsing to her knees. Max is still shocked.*

MAX: What is wrong with her?!
LIZ: (*struggling to hold Julie*) She wants to go back but she's afraid of what will happen when we do.
JULIE: (*sobbing, stops struggling with Liz*) We've all lost our jobs, and who knows what else. We've lost everything, thanks to this Pete character.
MAX: So we can't go back. So what? As far as I'm concerned, that's a good thing. Look at how beautiful it is here. We're making music whenever we feel like it. This place is paradise!
JULIE: It might be paradise to you. You two spend all your time in bed with each other.
MAX: And making music. We actually spend more time making music than in bed.
LIZ: That's really why we're here, Julie -- to make music! Making love is a bonus.
JULIE: Lust is not a valid substitute for corporate civilization.
MAX: Lust? What about love?
LIZ: Yes. What about love? Max and I love each other. I know that much, at least.
JULIE: Love is a myth from the past. Is love flesh tangled together in a bed? Corporate scientists consider love a throw back emotion, left over from the days before Chemical Emancipation.
MAX: You don't believe that, Julie, and you know it. Liz and I love each other.
JULIE: How can you be so sure?

MAX: Love is one of those . . .

> *Max pauses, searching for a word. Liz whispers in his ear. He listens, nods in agreement.*

MAX: . . . things.

> *Max and Liz sing:*

SONG: **BABY, THIS IS REALLY LOVE** (*duet*)

MAX:
> LOVE REALLY IS THE STRANGEST WORD,
> IT DIES UNSPOKEN, SOARS WHEN HEARD.
> LOVE CAN MAKE THE WEAK FEEL STRONG,
> CAN MAKE THE SILENT SING A SONG.
> SOME FOLKS WILL SAY THUS AND SO,

LIZ:
> WHAT DO THOSE FOLKS REALLY KNOW?

MAX & LIZ:
> I SWEAR BY STARS SO HIGH ABOVE
> THAT BABY, THIS IS REALLY LOVE.

LIZ:
> THIS LOVE OF MINE'S GOT ME IN A TIZZY,
> WINDMILLS THEY ALL LOOK DIZZY.
> AND MY HAIR'S ALL GONE FRIZZY,
> 'CAUSE BABY THIS IS REALLY LOVE.

MAX & LIZ:
> IF THIS AIN'T LOVE, JESSE JAMES WAS A GIRL
> AND FISH ARE WALKING TALL.
> BALLET DANCERS NEVER TWIRL,
> AND ELEPHANTS ARE SMALL.

MAX:
> LOVE MIGHT SEEM A BIT INSANE,
> THE WAY IT TENDS TO WAX AND WANE.

LIZ:
>I HARDLY KNOW HOW TO EXPLAIN,

MAX & LIZ:
>BUT HONEY THIS IS REALLY LOVE.
>
>SOME FOLKS CALL A SHRIMP A PRAWN,
>COCKS OR ROOSTERS CROW AT DAWN.
>JUST DON'T YOU SAY PERHAPS OR MAYBE,
>THIS IS REALLY LOVE, BABY.

MAX:
>LAST IS LAST

LIZ:
>AND FIRST IS FIRST

MAX:
>BEST IS BEST

LIZ:
>AND WORST IS WORST

MAX:
>SOME MIGHT SAY THAT I'VE BEEN CURSED.

LIZ:
>BUT BABY IT'S ONLY LOVE.

MAX:
>IF THIS AIN'T LOVE EV'RY FROG IS A KING,
>AND DARKNESS SHINES SO BRIGHT.

LIZ:
>EV'RY STONE'S A DIAMOND RING,
>CATS AND DOGS DON'T FIGHT.

MAX & LIZ:
>SOME FOLKS CLAIM THEY'RE IN THE KNOW,
>HAVE THEY FELT THEIR HEARTS AGLOW?
>I SWEAR BY ALL THE STARS ABOVE,
>THAT BABY THIS IS REALLY,
>BABY THIS IS REALLY,
>BABY THIS IS REALLY LOVE.
>>*End of song*

MAX: There it is, Julie. Love isn't a condition. Love is the truth.
LIZ: (*interjecting, cutting off Max*) That's it! Mister Max, get out the fishing gear and go do your duty. Julie can relax while I get a fire started, then we can go for a walk.
JULIE: How come you're so good at all this?
LIZ: It's not that I'm so good at it. It's that you're so bad.
JULIE: But where did you learn it all? How did you learn to start a fire?
LIZ: I lit a match.

> *Pete enters dressed in his golden jumpsuit.*

PETE: Aloha! Did you miss me?
JULIE: Pete! You're back. Oh yes! Yes! I missed you. We all missed you! We're so happy to see you!

> *Julie rushes to Pete, throws her arms around him, kisses him repeatedly on his face and neck.*

PETE: (*chuckles, disengages from embrace*) Well, it's certainly nice to feel welcome.
LIZ: Hi, Pete!
JULIE: When are we going back to civilization?!
PETE: Is tomorrow soon enough for you?
JULIE: Tomorrow is perfect! I'm going to go get ready.

> *Julie exits.*

MAX: (*sighs*) There goes my threesome.
PETE: You're not going back to your previous petty lives. You'll spend the next month at Corporate Headquarters.

UKULELE LAND

LIZ: Corporate Headquarters?!?
MAX: Why?
PETE: There's an orientation program before you go out on the road and appear in front of general audiences.
LIZ: You mean the Top Ten? You mean we're going to be in the Top Ten?
MAX: We're not ready yet, Pete. We need more time to practice. Please, just a little more time. Listen to this new song.

Max sings:

SONG: ***UKULELE BEACH BUM*** (*fragment*)

MAX:
>I'M JUST A UKULELE BEACH BUM
>AS HAPPY AS I CAN BE
>ANY SANDY BEACH OR SHADY PALM
>IS HOME SWEET HOME TO ME

Pete cuts off the singing.

PETE: (*interrupting*) Yes yes. Very nice.
MAX: It will be a great tune with a little more practice.
PETE: For the music you'll be playing? You've had plenty of practice.

END OF ACT ONE

THERE IS A DOOR PRIZE DRAWING
FOR A UKULELE
DURING INTERMISSION

ACT TWO

ACT TWO
SCENE 5: CORPORATE HQ

Two weeks later. Pete, in his golden jumpsuit, and Julie, dressed again in futuristic corporate costume, are alone. Julie has a golden ukulele. The Big Red © is on the backdrop. Pete and Julie sing:

SONG: ***YOU'VE GOT WHAT IT TAKES*** (*duet*)

JULIE:
> C'MON AND TELL ME WHAT'S YOUR PLAN?

PETE:
> ME? I WILL TRY TO DO ALL I CAN.

JULIE:
> YOU'RE TELLING ME
> THAT'S WHAT YOU CALL A PLAN?

Dancers enter and gather to listen.

PETE:
> PLAN? I'M THE MAN
> AND YOU KNOW I'M YOUR BIGGEST FAN.
> YOU CAN BE THE QUEEN OF POP,
> YOU'LL REACH THE TOP WITHOUT A STOP.

JULIE:
> BUT YOU KNOW I'M THE ONE
> WHO ALWAYS MAKES MISTAKES.

PETE:
> YOU'RE THE ONE WHO'S GOING
> TO GET ALL THE BREAKS,
> I CAN PROMISE YOU
> THAT THERE'LL BE NO HEARTACHES,
> 'CAUSE YOU'VE GOT WHAT IT TAKES.

A big dance number takes place.

PETE:
>WHEN YOU'RE HOT, YOU'LL BE SO COOL.

JULIE:
>WHAT IF I LOOK LIKE A FOOL.

PETE:
>C'MON KID, YOU WERE BORN TO RULE,

JULIE:
>YOU KNOW THAT WOULD
>REALLY BE SUPER COOL,

PETE:
>I KNOW YOU'VE GOT WHAT IT TAKES
>TO OUTSHINE ALL THE FLAKES AND FAKES,

JULIE:
>I'LL BE PLAYING
>FOR THE VERY HIGHEST STAKES,
>THAT GIVES ME THE QUAKY SHAKES,

PETE:
>I CAN PROMISE YOU
>THAT THERE'LL BE NO HEARTACHES,

JULIE: (*spoken*) I got it!

PETE & ENSEMBLE: (*sing*)
>YOU'VE I'VE GOT WHAT IT TAKES!
>*End of song*

>*Captain of the Guard enters.*

CAPTAIN: What's going on here? Who authorized singing and dancing?
PETE: I did. Just a little fun.
CAPTAIN: These people are on duty!

>*Pete shrugs, dismissive. He and Julie begin to bill and coo.*

CAPTAIN: Detail, 'ten hut!

> *Dancers revert to Corporate Security mode and exit with the Captain.*

PETE: That new uke makes you sound better than ever, Julie. And the color is certainly right, for you. I just hope your band mates can live up to their new ukes.
JULIE: Pete, you've got to get off this kick about Liz and Max. I'm sticking with my band.
PETE: Your loyalty to your friends is admirable. I hope someday you feel that strongly about me.
JULIE: Oh, Pete . . . Wait a minute! Are you saying all this because we've been sleeping together? If that's what this is about, then listen up.

> *Julie sings:*

SONG: ***COME SHAKE ALONG WITH ME***

JULIE:
>EVERY ONE TALKS ABOUT REAL TRUE LOVE,
>AS THOUGH IT'S MAGIC
>OR A GIFT FROM ABOVE.
>BUT THAT KIND OF TALK
>REALLY MAKES ME FEEL BLUE,
>SO HERE'S A THOUGHT
>ABOUT LOVE JUST FOR YOU.
>
>DON'T MISTAKE WHAT YOU'RE MAKIN'
>WHEN YOU'RE MAKIN' IT WITH ME.
>PLEASE DON'T THINK WHAT YOU'RE TAKIN'
>GROWS ON SOME SILLY LOVE TREE.

UKULELE LAND

THERE ARE LIMITS TO EV'RY KISS,
EVEN KISSES THAT TASTE LIKE SMILES.
LOVE'S FOR LOVERS AND LOVERS MISS
FLEXING THEIR FABULOUS WILES.

I DON'T WANT NO EMOTIONAL TRIAL.
FOREVER ONLY LASTS FOR AWHILE.
DON'T MISTAKE WHAT YOU'RE MAKIN'
WHEN YOU'RE MAKIN' IT WITH ME.
SO IF YOU SEE ME SHAKIN',
STOP HESITATIN',
AND COME ALONG WITH ME.
    End of song

PETE: Julie, it has nothing to do with us. You're going on the road soon and we won't see each other for months. My concern is for you -- that you don't make a mistake.

JULIE: I'm not making a mistake.

PETE: You're okay with the song I gave you?

JULIE: Pete, you heard us do it. We're fine. I'm still not sure why we're doing that song. It's really not our style at all. But if you say . . .

PETE: It's the sound that's hot right now. It's also got a solid message reinforcing corporate values. And singing it helps me. I helped you. Now you help me. Is that so much to ask?

JULIE: No no. We'll sing it. But, how does it help you? You were already in the Top 10.

PETE: That was (*pause*) a long time ago, Julie. My music was forgotten. Having a hot new band cover one of my tunes gives me juice.

JULIE: Juice?

PETE: Power. Position. The things that protect you. Please sing my song.

JULIE: How big will the audience be tomorrow? We've only ever played for each other.
PETE: And for me. Just pretend I'm the only one out there when you start.
JULIE: It's exciting. And nerve wracking. I'd better go practice.
PETE: Will I see you tonight?

> *Julie throws her arms around Pete, kisses him.*

JULIE: If that's what you really want, Pete, I could be there.

> *Julie exits, then Pete sings:*

SONG: ***THE BET***

PETE:

> I HAVE BET MY LIFE ON YOU
> ODD, BUT IT FEELS NICE
> YOU CAN MAKE IT ALL COME TRUE
> COME ON, LADY, ROLL THE DICE
> WIN US A TRIP TO PARADISE
>
> LOVE MAKES ME FEEL FUNNY
> MUST IT DRIVE ME INSANE?
> LIKE A BEAR THAT LOVES HIS HONEY
> I'M LONGING TO GET STUNG AGAIN
>
> NOW THAT I HAVE COME THIS FAR
> THE BEST IS IN SIGHT
> LET ME WISH UPON A STAR
> PLEASE, MY LADY, MAKE IT RIGHT
> I'M HUNGRY FOR YOUR LOVE TONIGHT

UKULELE LAND

WHEN WILL LOVE AND MONEY
POUR DOWN ON ME LIKE RAIN?
DOES A BEAR THAT LOVES HIS HONEY
 THINK SWEETNESS ALWAYS
COMES WITH PAIN?

I HAVE BET MY LIFE ON YOU
ODD, BUT IT FEELS NICE
YOU CAN MAKE IT ALL COME TRUE
COME ON, LADY, ROLL THE DICE
WIN US A TRIP TO PARADISE
WIN US A TRIP TO PARADISE
  End of song

SCENE 6: BACKSTAGE

Backstage at Corporate Headquarters Executive Auditorium, the lights come up on Liz, Max, and Julie, with ukes in hand. The ukes are the same golden color as Pete's jumpsuit.

JULIE: Look, we're singing Pete's song. Okay? We want to get into the Top Ten, right? So we're singing the song.

MAX: Sure. We're "singing" the song. Whatever. You and Pete are monogamous, aren't you? That's what this is all about, isn't it?

JULIE: We slept together a couple times, not that it's any of your business.

MAX: I knew it!

LIZ: Max, you just figured this out?

JULIE: What is the big deal? You both told me Pete was lusting after me and if that's what it takes, that's what it takes. (*pause*) Well, he took.

MAX: So, welcome to the revolution.

LIZ: Come on. Big band hug.

Liz gathers them both with her arms. The trio huddles in an embrace.

MAX, LIZ, & JULIE: (*in unison*) To the top together!
MAX: With ukuleles and lots of hot monogamy!

SCENE 7: ON STAGE IN AUDITORIUM
A singer stands at center stage and sings:

SONG: ***I'M ME***

SINGER:
>NOW MY TIME HAS COME AND I SHALL RISE,
>BRIGHT LIKE THE SUN IN THE MORNING,
>AND MY HEARTFELT SONG, IT WILL BE SUNG
>GRAND LIKE A STORM WITHOUT WARNING,
>
>THERE'S NOTHING MORE
>THAT CAN EVER STOP ME.
>THIS IS MY LIFE FILLED WITH JOY,
>BRIGHT NEW DAY, IT'S MY WAY.
>
>I KNOW MY PATH IS RIGHT,
>I'LL SHOW MY LIGHT,
>IT CAN'T BE WRONG.
>NOW, MY LIFE IS MINE,
>MY SOUL WILL SHINE,
>FOR I AM STRONG.
>THIS IS THE TRUTH THAT HAS SET ME FREE.
>I KNOW THAT I CAN BE ME.
>>*End of song*
>
>>*Canned applause*
>>*Applause ends by being cut off by a loud electronic buzz and the neon image of a huge red neon "Thumb Down" flashes off and on.*

ANNOUNCER'S VOICE: (*over action*) Music that attempts to inspire individuality will not be tolerated in the Top 10. Security, please start the process to lead this misguided individual into chemical emancipation.

> *Security forces enter. The singer is grabbed and is taken offstage, struggling against his fate.*

SINGER: No! Wait! They liked it! Don't do this! They were clapping, dammit. They were clapping.
ANNOUNCER'S VOICE: And now, on to our next act. This trio is our latest and best candidate for the Top 10. Let's give a very warm and hearty corporate welcome to The Ukulele Outlaws!!!

> *Canned Applause is heard as the trio enters, each with a golden ukulele, and they sing the first few words to the accompaniment of the ukes. The trio sings:*

SONG: *I WANNA BE A DRUG*

MAX, LIZ, & JULIE:
> I WANNA BE A DRUG
> I WANNA BE YOUR FAV 'RITE MED
> I WANNA BE A DRUG
> I WANNA GET INSIDE YOUR HEAD

> *Music makes a drastic change to Pop rock. The trio occasionally strums a chord on their ukes.*

JULIE:
> I WANNA BE A DRUG
MAX & LIZ:
> CRAVE ME, CRAVE ME, CRAVE.
JULIE:
> I WANNA BE A DRUG
MAX & LIZ:
> NEED ME, NEED ME, NEED.

JULIE:
>I WANNA BE A DRUG

MAX & LIZ:
>CRAVE ME, CRAVE ME, CRAVE.

JULIE:
>I WANNA BE A DRUG

MAX & LIZ:
>NEED ME, NEED ME, NEED.

MAX:
>I WANNA BE A DRUG FOR YOU.
>I WANNA GET INSIDE YOUR HEAD.
>I WANNA BE A DRUG FOR YOU.
>I WANNA BE YOUR FAV-RITE MED.

>*A big flashing green neon "Thumbs Up" Dancers enter.*

JULIE:
>I WANNA BE A DRUG

MAX & LIZ:
>CRAVE ME, CRAVE ME, CRAVE.

JULIE:
>I WANNA BE A DRUG

MAX & LIZ:
>NEED ME, NEED ME, NEED.

JULIE:
>I WANNA BE A DRUG

MAX & LIZ:
>CRAVE ME, CRAVE ME, CRAVE.

JULIE:
>I WANNA BE A DRUG

MAX & LIZ:
>NEED ME, NEED ME, NEED.

>*Trio exits at a run.*

DANCERS:
>I WANNA BE A DRUG FOR YOU.
>I WANNA CURE YOUR ACHES AND PAINS.
>I WANNA BE A DRUG FOR YOU.
>I WANNA GURGLE THROUGH YOUR VEINS.

>>*The trio enters, now wearing their golden jumpsuits. Julie and Liz both wear spiked blonde wigs.*

JULIE:
>I WANNA BE A DRUG
MAX & LIZ:
>CRAVE ME, CRAVE ME, CRAVE.
JULIE:
>I WANNA BE A DRUG
MAX & LIZ:
>NEED ME, NEED ME, NEED.
JULIE:
>I WANNA BE A DRUG
MAX & LIZ:
>CRAVE ME, CRAVE ME, CRAVE.
JULIE:
>I WANNA BE A DRUG
MAX & LIZ:
>NEED ME, NEED ME, NEED.
ALL:
>I WANNA BE A DRUG, I WANNA BE A DRUG,
>I WANNA BE A DRUG, I WANNA BE A DRUG.
>I WANNA BE A DRUG, I WANNA BE A DRUG,
>I WANNA BE A DRUG, I WANNA BE A DRUG.
JULIE:
>I WANNA BE A DRUG
MAX :
>CRAVE ME, CRAVE ME, CRAVE.

JULIE:
>I WANNA BE A DRUG

MAX:
>NEED ME, NEED ME, NEED.

LIZ:
>I WANNA BE A DRUG

MAX:
>CRAVE ME, CRAVE ME, CRAVE.

JULIE:
>I WANNA BE A DRUG

MAX:
>NEED ME, NEED ME, NEED.

ALL:
>WANNA, WANNA, WANNA, WANNA, WANNA,
>WANNA, WANNA, WANNA, WANNA, WANNA,
>WANNA, WANNA, WANNA, WANNA, WANNA,
>WANNA, WANNA, WANNA, WANNA, WANNA,
>WANNA, WANNA, WANNA, WANNA, WANNA,
>WANNA, WANNA, WANNA, WANNA, WANNA,
>WANNA, WANNA

JULIE:
>BE A DRUG, BE A DRUG, BE A DRUG, BE A
>DRUG, BE A DRUG, BE A DRUG, BE A DRUG,
>BE A DRUG, BE A DRUG, BE A DRUG,
>BE A DRUG, BE A DRUG, BE A DRUG,
>BE A DRUG, BE A DRUG, BE A DRUG.
>>*End of song*

SCENE 8: CORPORATE HQ

Neon flashing: One year later.
Pete, wearing his gold jumpsuit, stands at center stage. The trio enters wearing their gold jumpsuits. They spot Pete, cross to him.

MAX, LIZ, & JULIE: (*variously*) Hey, Hey, Hey Pete. What's up? Aloha, dude? Great to see you. You're looking at some road dogs now. Yeaahh Baby!
PETE: Wow! Great to see you kids. It's been too long. A year – can you believe it? And congratulations are in order. *I Wanna Be A Drug* is Number 1 on the charts again this week. That's ten weeks in a row!
MAX: It's good to be number one!
JULIE: Go ahead. Tell him.
PETE: Tell me what?
MAX: You tell him, Liz..
LIZ: No - you.
MAX: C'mon baby.
LIZ: (*squeals with delight*) We're getting married!
MAX: Now that we're in the Top 10, we're going monogamous.
PETE: Wait a minute. You want to repeat that??
MAX: Now that we're . . .
LIZ: Max and I are getting married! We want a big wedding! We're going to invite all the media.
PETE: Monogamous? Marriage?! Are you trying to start a revolution?
MAX: Ummm, yeah! Absolutely. Once we're in the Top 10 we can do whatever we want. That's the deal, right? Otherwise, what's the point? Well, Liz and I want to get married -- to each other. We're going to set an outlaw example.
PETE: Wow. Well, that will be different. But sure. I guess. You can do whatever you want. And Julie. How about you?

UKULELE LAND

JULIE: (*hesitantly*) Well, I met a guy awhile ago. I'm pretty sure he's the one. Until we get together again, though, I'm concentrating on our music, and on helping these two get ready for their big day.
MAX: Speaking of which, we should go, ladies. We've got a wedding to plan.

> *Pete turns away, in thought. Liz and Max exit. Julie follows a few steps.*

JULIE: (*calls after them*) I'll catch up with you in a few. Ciao.

> *Julie turns, crosses toward Pete.*

JULIE: Umm, Pete, could we talk?
PETE: (*startled from his reverie*) Julie?! Oh sure. Hi.
JULIE: I can come back later if that's better.
PETE: No. Now is fine. What's up?
JULIE: Well this is going to sound strange . . . Oh, never mind.
PETE: Wait, Julie. Tell me.
JULIE: (*turns back*) Pete, I missed you! The whole time I was gone I missed you.
PETE: But you said you met someone.
JULIE: I did. I met you, Pete. I missed you. I really really missed you.
PETE: Wow! You missed me?
JULIE: Of course I did. You never called me the whole time we were on the road. No text. No communication of any kind. Nothing. Not a word from you.

> *Julie and Pete embrace. Suddenly a sharp electronic buzz is heard and the Love Police, led by the Captain of the Guard, march on stage and surround the couple. They cling,*

then are dragged apart. Two guards each grab Pete by an elbow.

CAPTAIN: You are now officially in our custody.

Pete's shoulders sag and he hangs his head and stares at the ground.

JULIE: What? Wait just a minute! This man wears the golden jumpsuit! Do you know who this man is?
CAPTAIN: I know that he's not who he claims. I've been investigating him for a year now. He was never part of the Top Ten. He's not entitled to wear the golden jumpsuit. This man is an imposter!

SCENE 9: SPOT SCENE
Julie is sobbing, Liz and Max stare.

MAX: (*loudly*) Calm down, Julie! Tell us exactly what happened.
JULIE: (*sobbing*) Corporate security (*sob*) they took him away (*sob*) just after we said we loved each other.
LIZ: They took him away because you said you loved each other?!
JULIE: No, no. That Captain said that Pete was never part of the Top Ten – that he was an imposter!
MAX: Wow!
LIZ: Pete's a fake?
MAX: Too much! He really was an edger.
LIZ: How'd he pull all this off then? How'd he get us our audition? We're still in the Top Ten, right? The Corporation can't take that away, can they? We're already stars. We have fans. We're Number One!
MAX: No way they can take that from us. We're too famous. But they can take Pete away and for good, the crazy Edger! Julie, you're so stupid. You fell for that nobody! You're better than that, bigger than that. He's just a waste of space.

SCENE 10: PRISON

Upstage, raised, Pete is behind bars wearing an orange prison jumpsuit. Julie enters with a guard following closely. The guard carries a medical bag bearing the corporate © logo.

PETE: Julie!?! Where have you been?
JULIE: Where have I been?
PETE: What are you doing here? What's going on?

Guard hands Julie a huge syringe.

JULIE: What am I doing here? I've been granted permission to administer your first dose of reconstructive pharma therapy. I'm here to help you transition to chemical emancipation. That's what I'm doing. This is what I used to do, Pete. Before I met you. Before you came into our lives with all your lies!
PETE: Oh Julie, I'm so sorry about that.
JULIE: Sorry? You're so sorry?

Julie advances toward Pete, squirting liquid out of the end of the hypo with each step. Pete backs away from the bars of his cell.

GUARD: Hey! You're going to squirt it all out!

Julie turns and squirts another shot of the liquid.

JULIE: Oops! All gone. Go get me another! Right away!

Julie hands the hypo to Guard and points.

JULIE: Go!

Guard exits.

PETE: My darling! I thought you would. . .
JULIE: (*interrupting*) Knock it off Pete! Don't you 'my darling me.' I'm finished with your nonsense.
PETE: Julie, slow down and let me . . .
JULIE: (*interrupting again*) You lied to me! Why did you lie to me about everything? ...IMPOSTER! That's what you are alright!
PETE: (*almost in shock*) I only did that to get you into the Top Ten! So you could do your music, your wonderful music, Julie.
JULIE: Don't start with that 'wonderful music" garbage again and . . .
PETE: (*interrupting, angry*) You're the impostor! You and your little friends---you're selling out! Doing my crappy song over and over again. Where's your music?!
JULIE: You pushed us to do that song. You are the one who wrote it!
PETE: Are you kidding me? I only wrote that song so you could get into the Top Ten! That song has no melody...no harmony...no soul...NOTHING! (*sarcastically sings*) "I WANNA BE A DRUG, CRAVE ME, CRAVE ME, CRAVE ME." It's just noise, Julie.
JULIE: (*covering her ears*) I'm not listening to you anymore.
PETE: Okay, go ahead, be the corporation's little whore. The music doesn't matter to you anymore, huh Julie, now that you all have your shiny jumpsuits.
JULIE: Shut up, Pete! I hate you! I knew I should never have listened to you! Why did I ever get involved with you?
PETE: You say I'm an imposter . . . but at least I know who I am. Look, Julie, I wasn't really in the Top Ten.
JULIE: Tell me something I don't know.

PETE: The day before I met you I found the gold jumpsuit in a dumpster behind the funeral center. I grabbed it, figuring maybe I could sell it. Then, when Corporate Security stormed in on you that first night, I saw that I might be able to use it to lead them away from you. I put it on and walked right out there like I was a big shot and they followed me, like the idiots they are. (*pause*) I waltzed into an empty office and claimed it, made it mine, and no one even noticed. No one even did a background check on me.
JULIE: I can't believe all this happened because of a silly gold jumpsuit.
PETE: Did you know the golden jumpsuit is indestructible? I think whoever owned mine previously was cremated in it. That's how it ended up . . .
JULIE: Enough! You just have to keep it up don't you Pete; you just don't know when to stop!

Julie storms out. Then Pete sings:

SONG: ***LOVE'S CRIME***

PETE:
>SHE WAS NEVER MINE,
>BUT HOW WE LOVED
>FOR SUCH A SHORT TIME.
>HOW CAN I SAY GOODBYE?
>
>THE SUMMER SUN STILL SHINES,
>LOVING MUSIC WAS MY CRIME,
>MY HEART'S LOVE WILL WITHER AND DIE.
>
>AND TRY AS I MIGHT
>TO MAKE THINGS ALL RIGHT,
>BUT THE WATERS OF LOVE RUN DRY.
>DRY SAND IN MY HEART

UKULELE LAND

WHERE RIVERS SHOULD START,
A NOW BROKEN LOVER AM I,

REGARDLESS OF SEASON,
LOVE BLOOMS WITHOUT REASON,
AND FLOATS AWAY ON A SIGH.
>   *End of song*

SCENE 11: BACKSTAGE AT A CONCERT ARENA

Max is pacing, getting ready to go on stage. Julie enters.

MAX: (*very irritated*) Julie you're late, we're going on in 20 minutes; where have you been? Our first worldwide broadcast...the corporation finally trusts us enough to do a LIVE simulcast-
JULIE: (*corrects pronunciation*) Simulcast.
MAX: Simulcast? Really? (*continues as before*) Anyway, you just take off and disappear on us?

Liz enters but doesn't see Julie right away.

LIZ: (*mad with excitement*) Max, you're right! The stadium is already packed. This is unbelievable! I've never seen so many people in one place. The Ukulele Outlaws! (*giddy*) Soon every girl in the world will want to look EXACTLY LIKE ME! I mean, is that FABULOUS or WHAT?! (*sees Julie*) Julie!
MAX: Liz, our Julie here, on our biggest day -- SHE's off hanging around that loser Pete.
JULIE: (*exhausted*) Yeah, he's a loser, alright. You should have heard the story he gave me.
LIZ: Julie, don't talk that way about Pete. Would we be in the Top Ten without his help?
JULIE: Now, thinking about it, I can almost believe that stupid story of his. You know, he did explain his gold jumpsuit and that office of his. (*pause*) The thing is, he sounded like he was really serious. It was just so upsetting seeing him locked up like that. (*recognizing the full truth*) Oh WOW! He actually put his life on the line so we could play our music...and now he'll be locked up forever!
LIZ: Yeah, forever. He's going to be in the prison hospital getting pharmed out of his mind. There won't be anything left of the real Pete.

JULIE: Pete is right, though – we're imposters too.
MAX: Now what's that supposed to mean?
JULIE: It means we're not playing our music, at all! That's what it means. It means we're sell outs to the corporation.

> *They all stop short. Long pause. The trio looks at each other and, as one, signify as one that they understand what they have to do.*

SCENE 12: ARENA STAGE
Music for "I Wanna be a Drug" starts.

ANNOUNCER: And now, ladies and gentlemen, the Ukulele Outlaws!

> *Trio enters with their ukes. They stand with arms folded across their ukes until the music stops. Liz and Julie take off their wigs and toss them aside. Max holds up his hand. The music stops.*

MAX: Give me a vamp in F, please.

> *Liz and Julie vamp on their ukes. The trio sings:*

SONG: ***UKULELE LAND*** (*reprise*)

> UKULELE LAND, THAT'S THE PLACE TO BE.
> UKULELE LAND, ALL YOUR CARES WILL FLEE.
> HOT PEPPER CHILI AND HAWAIIAN SHIRTS.
> UKULELE LAND, WHERE LOVE NEVER HURTS.

> *Neon palm trees, sun, argon clouds, slide in on the backdrop. Two huge Tiki figures with glowing red eyes, breathing smoke, rise from the floor. The words UKULELE LAND start flashing. Dancers enter in grass skirts and leis.*

> UKULELE LAND, SKIES ARE ALWAYS BLUE,
> UKULELE LAND, FRIENDS ARE ALWAYS TRUE.
> FREEDOM RINGS OUT DAILY,
> FROM EV'RY UKULELE.
> UKULELE LAND, THAT'S THE PLACE TO BE.

UKULELE LAND

UKULELE LAND, FIRES ON THE BEACH.
UKULELE LAND, NOTHING'S OUT OF REACH.
YOU'LL LEARN GIN RUMMY
AND GORGE AT HOT CLAM BAKES,
PLAYING UKULELE,
THAT'S ALL THAT IT TAKES.

UKULELE LAND, DANCING IN GRASS SKIRTS.
ALL THAT YOU CAN EAT
OF THOSE CHOC'LATE DESSERTS.
SLEEP ALL DAY, NIGHTS RUN WILD,
YOU WILL FIND YOUR INNER CHILD.
UKULELE LAND,
THAT'S WHERE YOU'LL WANNA BE,

> *The dancers join in singing. Upstage, raised, prison bars appear. Pete and 4 or 5 supernumeraries are behind the bars. One of the Love Police enters with a comically huge key, hands it thru the bars to Pete, then skips off. Pete unlocks the cell. All behind bars now step into freedom. Supernumeraries exit in one direction, Pete exits opposite.*

ALL:
UKULELE LAND, CROWDS ALL SING ALONG
UKULELE LAND, YOU'LL KNOW EVERY SONG.
ALL KINDS OF DANCERS
SWINGIN' CHEEK TO CHEEK,
YOU CAN EVEN EARN
A MILLION BUCKS A WEEK.

UKULELE LAND, EV'RYONE IS KIND,
PLAY THAT UKULELE,
NOT A SOUL WILL MIND.

STRUM THAT UKULELE
AND SING YOUR LOVE SONGS GAILY.
UKULELE LAND, THAT'S THE PLACE TO BE.
    End of song

SCENE 13: THE WRAP-UP WEDDING, ALL THINGS HAPPY

The trio stands near the very front of the stage. Upstage dancers run to and fro, waving as they pass each other, stopping occasionally to shake hands or hug. Pete enters wearing Hawaiian shirt and crosses to the trio.

PETE: Aloha, kids!
JULIE: Pete, you're free!

Hugs all around.

PETE: Everyone's free! There's a ukulele revolution going on, thanks to the music of The Ukulele Outlaws! The Love Police all started humming and whistling Ukulele Land and they let all the drug evaders out of prison.
MAX: I can't believe it. Our music really did start a revolution. And it is our music (*to Pete*). All our music, Pete. Just like it should be. We sang Ukulele Land, but it's your song.
PETE: Thanks Max. That means a lot to me.
JULIE: You mean a lot to me.
PETE: C'mon, Baby, let's monogamate. Hot Cha Cha!

Julie and Pete kiss and hug. Max taps Pete on the shoulder and hands him a uke.

MAX: Do you remember this tune, Pete?

Max starts strumming, and they all sing:

SONG: *UKULELE BEACH BUM /*
UKULELE BEACHBABE (entire song reprise)

PETE and MAX:
>I'M JUST A UKULELE BEACH BUM
>AS HAPPY AS I CAN BE
>ANY SANDY BEACH OR SHADY PALM
>IS HOME SWEET HOME TO ME
>
>I HAVE NO CARES
>LIKE BILLIONAIRES
>NO GREED TO MAKE ME BLUE
>I PLAY UKULELE
>AND BREATHE FRESH AIR
>YEAH, THAT IS ALL I DO

JULIE and LIZ:
>UKULELE
>UKULELE
>UKULELE

PETE and MAX:
>I'M GOING BACK TO THAT SUNNY ISLE
>AND STAY PUT ALL MY LIFE
>IF SOME SWEET GAL
>WANTS A GOOD GUY
>SHE CAN BE MY WIFE
>
>I KNOW I'LL MAKE HER HAPPY
>UKULELE LOVIN' ALL THE TIME
>I HOPE THAT GAL'S A BILLIONAIRE
>'CAUSE I AIN'T GOT A DIME
>YEAH I HOPE THAT GAL'S A BILLIONAIRE
>'CAUSE I AIN'T GOT A DIME

UKULELE LAND

JULIE and LIZ:
> UKULELE
> UKULELE
> UKULELE

Julie and Liz start strumming their ukes.

JULIE and LIZ:
> I'M JUST A UKULELE BEACH BABE
> AS HAPPY AS I CAN BE
> ANY SANDY BEACH OR SHADY PALM
> IS HOME SWEET HOME TO ME
>
> I HAVE NO CARES
> LIKE BILLIONAIRES
> NO GREED TO MAKE ME BLUE
> I GO TO THE BEACH EVERY DAY
> PLAY UKULELE THAT'S ALL I DO

PETE and MAX:
> UKULELE
> UKULELE
> UKULELE

JULIE and LIZ:
> I'M GOING BACK TO THAT SUNNY ISLE
> TO STAY PUT ALL MY LIFE
> IF SOME SWEET GUY
> WANTS A GOOD GAL
> I CAN BE HIS WIFE
> I KNOW I'LL MAKE HIM HAPPY
> UKULELE LOVIN' ALL THE TIME
> I HOPE THAT GUY'S A BILLIONAIRE
> 'CAUSE I AIN'T GOT A DIME
> YEAH, I HOPE THAT GUY'S A BILLIONAIRE
> 'CAUSE I AIN'T GOT A DIME

PETE, MAX, JULIE and LIZ:
>UKULELE
>UKULELE
>UKULELE
>>*End of song*

>*Traditional wedding music as Chorus enters and dresses the quartet with wedding veils, golden top hats, and bouquets for the brides. The Quartet faces an unseen officiary.*

MAX: I do.
LIZ: I will.
PETE: I will.
JULIE: I DO.

>*Each couple kisses. The brides toss the bouquets over their shoulders.*

UKULELE LAND

SCENE 14: FINALE

Bucket-brigade-style line forms with dancers and principals. While singing, ukuleles are handed down the line until everyone has one. Cast sings:

SONG: ***WHAT IS IT 'BOUT MUSIC?***

JULIE:
> WHAT IS IT 'BOUT MUSIC?

PETE:
> WHAT IS IT 'BOUT MUSIC?

MAX and LIZ:
> WHAT IS IT 'BOUT MUSIC?

CAST:
> WHAT IS IT 'BOUT MUSIC?
> WHAT IS IT 'BOUT MUSIC?

LIZ:
> IT SETS YOUR SOUL FREE,
> MAKES YOUR CARES FLEE.

ALL:
> WHAT IS IT 'BOUT MUSIC?

JULIE:
> MAKES YOU SING ALONG,
> WHEN YOU HEAR THAT SONG.

MAX:
> AND WHEN YOU HEAR RHYTHM
> IT MOVES YOUR FEET,
> CAN'T BE BEAT

PETE:
> THAT SWEET MELODY
> LINGERS IN YOUR HEART,
> FROM THE START.

MAX and LIZ:
> WHAT IS IT 'BOUT MUSIC?

LIZ:
>BINDS A GIRL AND A BOY
>FILLED WITH JOY.

PETE/JULIE:
>WHAT IS IT MAKES MUSIC
>SO SWEET AND NEAT.

LIZ:
>MAKES DULL WORDS BRIGHT,

JULIE:
>LIGHTS UP THE NIGHT.

MAX:
>MAKES DANCERS ARCH

PETE:
>AND SOLDIERS MARCH,

PETE, LIZ, JULIE, MAX:
>WONDER WHAT THE MAGIC
>IN MUSIC CAN BE.

Uke strumming during dance break.

MAX:
>WHAT IS IT 'BOUT MUSIC?
>WHY'S IT REAL?
>TELL ME WHAT'S THE DEAL?

JULIE:
>WHAT IS IT 'BOUT MUSIC?
>MAKES A NEW TUNE WORK,

PETE:
>THAT'S THE KOOKY QUIRK.

MAX:
>YOU HEAR A GREAT MELODY,
>YOU CAN BET YOU WON'T FORGET.

LIZ:
>AND AFTER YOU'VE GONE TO BED,

PETE, LIZ, JULIE, MAX:
>THE SONG KEEPS PLAYIN' IN YOUR HEAD.
>WHAT IS IT 'BOUT MUSIC

MAX:
>PUTS THE RAZZMATAZZ
>AND THE JUMP IN JAZZ.

PETE, LIZ, JULIE, MAX:
>THAT MUSIC'S THE SOUL
>OF ANY SHOW WE KNOW.

LIZ:
>DRIES UP YOUR TEARS.

MAX:
>YES, WITH YOUR EARS.

PETE:
>SOOTHES THE RAGING HEART,
>RIPS FEAR APART.

ALL:
>GOOD MUSIC IS MAGIC FOR ME.
>*End of song*
>*Blackout*

VOTA: (*heard during blackout*)
>And so began the ukulele revolution that took music to every corner of the planet and made it all one monogomation nation. Now peace, freedom, happiness, love and laughter prevail and everywhere you hear the dreamy sweet strumming of the ukulele.

Curtain Call

Lights up. The Company reprises TIME TO FLY for the curtain call.

SONG: ***TIME TO FLY*** (*reprise*)

ALL:
>TAKE THE BLUE FROM THE SKY,
>PUT IT IN YOUR POCKET.
>TAKE YELLOW FROM THE SUN,
>FUEL UP THE ROCKET.
>WE'RE GONNA SOAR OUT THERE.
>MAKE ALL THE PEOPLE CARE,
>IT'S TIME TO FLY, IT'S TIME TO FLY.
>
>WHEN THERE'S TRUTH IN YOUR SONG,
>NO ONE CAN STOP YOU.
>IT SWINGS YOU RIGHT ALONG
>'TIL NO ONE CAN TOP YOU.
>PUT CHANCE IN YOUR ROMANCE,
>MAKE EV'RYBODY DANCE.
>IT'S TIME TO FLY, IT'S TIME TO FLY.
>
>TAKE THE BLUE FROM THE SKY,
>PUT IT IN YOUR POCKET.
>TAKE YELLOW FROM THE SUN,
>FUEL UP THE ROCKET.
>WE'RE GONNA SOAR OUT THERE.
>MAKE ALL THE PEOPLE CARE,
>IT'S TIME TO FLY, IT'S TIME TO FLY.

finis

ACKNOWLEDGMENTS

First, I want to thank the audiences who came to see the 2008 production.
My wife, Sara Jackson DiLauro, as always, was the shoulder I leaned on in more ways than one.
My son Jesse and my daughter Isabella were great cheerleaders for the project.
My parents also lent their unfailing support.
I also want to thank the staff at Theater for the New City, where the 2008 production was staged.
Thanks to Papa's Boxes for the cigar box ukuleles and to the Magic Fluke Company for the golden Fleas.
During the development of this musical, several creative souls joined the project and subsequently left. I thank them for their ideas, even though their efforts ended up on the proverbial "cutting room floor".
Spats White was part of the first developmental reading, and remained a friend and advisor every step of the way, and still does.
Jason Baruch gave me his sagacious and enthusiastic counsel.
My friends Dan Goldner and Geoff Rezek both made generous financial donations to the 2008 production.
Annie Pike lent her eyes to this print version as proof reader.
Finally, I must thank Charles de Bourbon of BGA Studios for the endless hours he put into *Ukulele Land*– editing video and sound, creating the website and graphics, and designing this edition.

I send all of you my thanks, appreciation, and love.

www.ingramcontent.com/pod-product-compliance
Lightning Source LLC
Chambersburg PA
CBHW031947070426
42453CB00007BA/489